Rupert's Adventures ~ Book C

Rupert Finds a Family

Lord Fritz III
Illustrations by Lisa Christie Leach

Eastern Reach Books

This book is a gift to

Camille

Given by

Great Grandma Patierno

On this date

November 5, 2022

Copyright © 2020 by Sinco B. Steendam

All rights reserved. No part of this publication may be reproduced, distributed or transmitted in any form or by any means, including photocopying, recording, or other electronic or mechanical methods, without the prior written permission of the publisher, except in the case of brief quotations embodied in critical reviews and certain other noncommercial uses permitted by copyright law. For permission requests, contact the publisher.

Eastern Reach Books
Wyoming, USA
www.easternreachbooks.com

Publisher's Note: This is a work of fiction. Names, characters, places, and incidents are a product of the author's imagination. Locales and public names are sometimes used for atmospheric purposes. Any resemblance to actual people, living or dead, or to businesses, companies, events, institutions, or locales is completely coincidental.

Original illustrations © Lisa Christie Leach
Edited by Rachel L. Hall
Book design © 2013, BookDesignTemplates.com; adapted by Rachel L. Hall

Rupert Finds a Family / Lord Fritz III— Second Edition

ISBN 978-0-9996503-0-1

Once upon a time, a smart, frisky squirrel lived in a big tree by a little yellow house.

Sometimes, he got into trouble.

One day, the squirrel saw a big truck pull up
to the little yellow house.

A new family was moving in.

"Each of you please help carry the small and medium boxes," said the Man with the Bow Tie.
"I will carry the big boxes."

The squirrel hid behind the big tree
and watched the family.

"Look, Mommy! A squirrel!" said Morgan. "He looks friendly."

Mrs. Maggie warned: "Be careful! Squirrels can bite."

"Daddy, I think the squirrel wants to be our friend," said Aaron.

"We don't have time for silly animals," said the Man with the Bow Tie. "We have lots of work to do. Keep that critter away from our door. We can't have a wild animal come in our new house."

And he said to the squirrel,
"Now, shoo!"

Back at the big tree, the squirrel sat and watched the
family move box after box out of the truck
and into the little yellow house.
But what was that? Something moved in the grass.

A snake! It slithered toward the house,
eyeing a bag of clothes near the front door.
To the snake, it looked like a nice, cozy place to explore.

The squirrel jumped up and down,
chattering loudly to warn the family.
But they were too busy moving their boxes to notice.

The squirrel had an idea.

"The squirrel has stolen our rope!" said the Man with the Bow Tie. "I just finished coiling it up. This squirrel is making me mad!"

The snake spotted the rope and went toward it.
Squirrel's idea was working!
But the family still did not see the snake.

The squirrel was quick. He tied the rope
to the white picket fence.
Snake slithered over to watch.

The family wondered, "What is the squirrel doing?"
The squirrel twirled the rope
and jumped and jumped.

Snake was not interested.
He turned to go.

The squirrel had another idea.
He ran and ran, here and there, back and forth,
in crazy circles with the rope.

"Look what the squirrel did!" said Alyssa.
"He tangled a snake in the rope!"

"The squirrel has saved us from the snake sneaking into our house!" said Luke.

"You're right, Luke. The squirrel was protecting us," said Mrs. Maggie.
The Man with the Bow Tie exclaimed, "Well, I'll be!"

"Mrs. Maggie, do we have some nuts to give our new friend?" asked the Man with the Bow Tie.

"He is a hero! We should give him a special name."
"Let's call him Rupert!" said Simon.

The whole family cheered for Rupert, their new, squirrely friend.

The End

Conversation Questions

1. Did you find Rupert's hidden acorns?
(Hint: there is one in every illustration!)

2. Why was Rupert sad? (pages 8–9)
Have you ever felt like that, too?

3. What did Rupert do to try and help the family?
(pages 12–21)

4. How did Rupert become a hero?

Take a Picture with Rupert!

Take a picture of this book being read and send it to RupertsAdventures2010@gmail.com

Once a month, submissions will be entered in a drawing.
The winner will receive a gift from Rupert.

DEDICATION

To my five grandchildren. You are the inspiration for the Rupert's Adventures series.

Simon, Alyssa, Luke, Rupert, Aaron & Morgan

Mrs. Maggie
&
The Man with the Bow Tie

The Author,
The Artist,
The Editor

Lord Fritz III is the brilliant goofball behind the Rupert's Adventures series. Rupert is forever looking over his shoulder to make sure he gets the stories right. Together, they want to make sure everybody remembers the importance of family values.

Lisa Christie Leach is the artsy doodler who attempts to capture Rupert's vast range of emotions in each picture. In her "spare" time she's the Director and Artist-in-Residence at Spirit Wind Center for Creativity & Healing in Stonington, Connecticut.

Rachel L. Hall is a freelance editor and sometime-book designer whose passion is capturing the frequency of her authors' hearts to ensure their messages reach readers in their intended form. But she's most proud of the four children she and husband are raising.

A Note From the Author

I have been inspired to create a "Rupert's culture" to promote family values and instill positive character qualities. The *Rupert's Adventures* book series will have a multi-faceted approach to teaching Kingdom priorities.

Children will love the zany adventures that Rupert the squirrel introduces to the loving family who adopts him.

Parents and teachers will see themselves in the adult characters and appreciate the message of integrity, character, love, and care they can share in a fun way with any kid they love.

10% of all *Rupert's Adventures* sales go to Radiant Destiny International, whose mission "to bring peace, hope and joy in very tangible ways to families in communities across the earth" is close the heart of the vision for this book series. Learn more at RadiantDestiny.com.

To find out more, visit EastgateOutreach.com and click on *Rupert's Adventures.*

Be sure to visit RupertsAdventures.com, too, and watch for new books to be released.

Made in the USA
Middletown, DE
21 August 2021